Watercolors and drawings by **Alain Bouldouyre**

Text by **Christophe Auduraud**

My Paris Sketchbook

Flammarion

Translated from the French by
Susan Pickford

Adapted by
Olivia McCannon

Copyediting by
Penelope Isaac and
Kimberley Conniff Taber

Proofreading by Slade Smith

Design by Emmanuel Laparra
for Gudul Prod

Typesetting by
Studio X-Act, Paris

Color separation by Eurésys

Originally published as
Mes Carnets de Paris
© 2002 Flammarion

Illustrations © Alain Bouldouyre

Text © Christophe Auduraud

English-language edition
© 2003 Flammarion

My Paris Sketchbook

Christophe Auduraud and Alain Bouldouyre

Flammarion

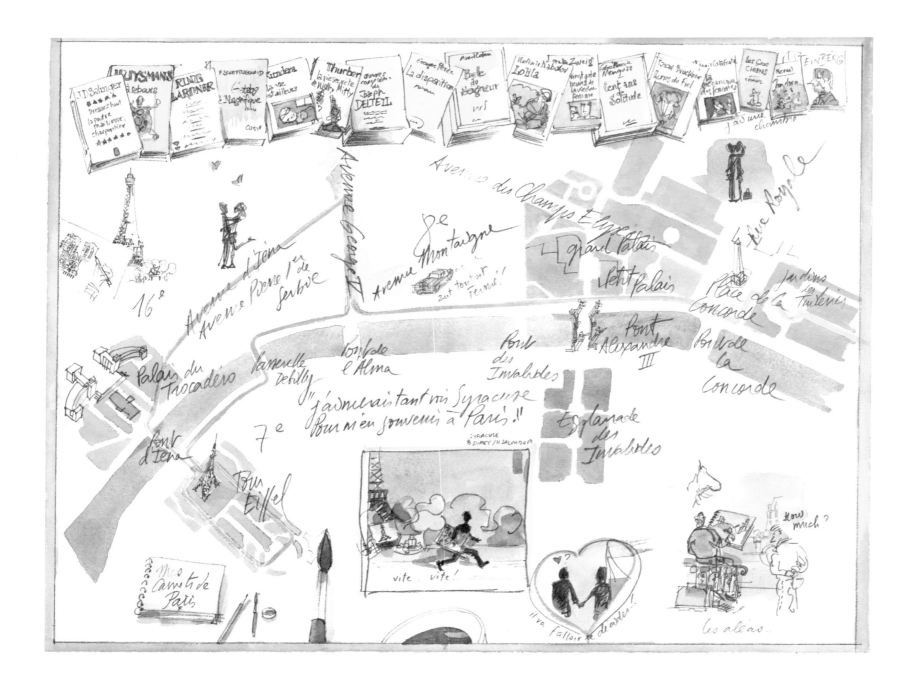

Contents

Doors and building façades on Avenue George-V, 8th arrondissement

Paris at Dawn

FROM RUE MARBEUF TO THE RITZ

It was a whim, a thirst for beauty, awoken by the vision of Paris drenched in sun...

Framed by my high window, the sun rises over the red chimney tops and zinc roofs, filling the spaces between the hazy domes and spires that shape the skyline. A new July day in the city. The street below is empty, poised for the first sign of movement.

Summer in Paris makes you itch to be outside, to stroll in and out of streets, turning corners toward shifting patches of sun or shade, your internal compass flicking east, north, west, south. It makes you want to wander, guided by no greater purpose than your next cup of coffee.

Parisians may not have invented *flânerie*, but they have made it their philosophy: walk to stay in the present, to be part of the life of the city and its flux of ideas, fashions, and moods. Walk, and keep your eyes open, *be* open to whatever crosses your path. To understand Paris, to change shape with Paris. Could this be one of the secrets to the city's eternal youth?

I step out into rue Marbeuf in the 8th arrondisement, where curved layers of cobblestones gleam like fish scales in the early morning sun. Here, the residents wake up in private, behind screens, curtains, and shutters, starting the day gently with trays of coffee, croissants, and newspapers. Later, their dogs will provide the pretext for a grand entrance onto the street via the shallow steps of a carpeted staircase or an elevator with a sliding ironwork grille, then out through a tiled entrance hall lined with mirrors.

I turn onto avenue Montaigne. The extravagantly-dressed mannequins are as haughty as ever—even at this hour they never let their mask of perfection slip, or relax those unnatural poses (so tiring to maintain), which reveal the details that make wealth desirable: embroidered buttons, the soft lining of a coat that slips on like a second skin, an ingenious asymmetrical cut.

I head down the chestnut tree-lined Champs-Élysées, where the traffic has already begun its crescendo into rush hour. I pause in front of the domed glass roof of the Grand Palais, and its smaller twin, both overlooking the Seine. These soaring metallic structures might be equally at home in a grandiose railway station. They caused some outcry when they rose up against the sky-line at the dawn of the twentieth century. But it's not the first, nor the last, architectural controversy to have left its enduring and endearing mark on the landscape of the city.

In the courtyard of the Grand Palais, I pause before Larche's sculpted representations of the Seine and its tributaries, reflected in

12

a mirror of water, displaying all the grace and sophistication of their era. Perfect for their riverside surroundings, they are a fitting homage to the central role played by the river in the past and present of Paris. I walk over to admire the Seine itself, a sinewy line dotted with barges and *bateaux mouches*, dividing Paris into two uneven halves.

This is the time of day when the sun glitters on golden domes, and makes the surface of the river shimmer like watered silk, or some other opulent fabric you might see dressing the windows of an important building. Like the Elysée Palace, for example, a little further north. As I pass the high walls and ranks of combat police, I wonder whether the French president may even now be holding an urgent briefing session with his senior ministers, after a night of international phone calls.

Not far away, on the rue du Faubourg Saint Honoré, men in crisp, sober uniforms guard the grand doorways of the embassies, whose flags gleam white in the sun. Behind each massive door is a vast courtyard housing reception rooms with leather armchairs to sink into. Should you make it past the guns, the glass screens, and the metal detectors, that is.

But this is also a road where, in the past, eccentricity has lived alongside officialdom. It is haunted by the self-indulgent spirits of a number of wealthy former inhabitants, including the first duke of Albuféra who trained his two parrots to sing Vespers and elevate the souls of passersby.

I intersect with a street leading down on my left and turn onto it, summoned by an imperious column pointing upwards like a finger. Jewelry Square, alias place Vendôme. This square belongs to those who do not know the meaning of "No". The endless glass cases—housing glittering diamonds and precious stones set into too-delicate or ostentatious gold designs—are like rows of candy jars to a child. All one has to do is point. No wonder the Communards demolished the column in 1871. No wonder it was re-erected in 1874. On the left-hand side of the square, the Ritz. One of those names. One of those hotels. Where the rooms are so grand their tall windows look down on the square. Where nothing may be refused. Where the silence is so expensive, the staff wear special shoes to make sure nothing mars it.

Where else could I go for breakfast, darling?

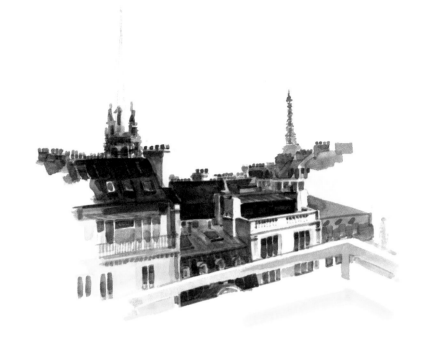

The sun rises over the red chimney tops and zinc roofs, filling the spaces between the hazy domes and spires that shape the skyline.

Charlotte, Rue de Washington. Paris 8e

Arriving at "Jewelry Square," place Vendôme

summer in Paris makes you itch to be
outside, to stroll in and out of streets,
turning corners towards shifting
patches of sun or shade...
It makes you want to wander, guided
by no greater purpose than your next
cup of coffee.

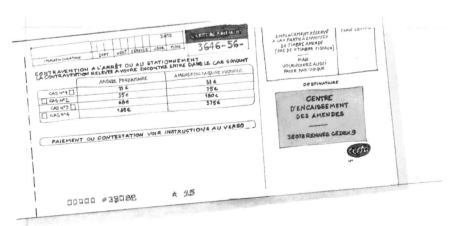

The Ritz... One of those names. One of those hotels,
where nothing may be refused...
where else could I go for breakfast?

Paris in the Morning

ALEXANDRE III BRIDGE TO NOTRE-DAME

Alexandre III Bridge

The Alexandre III Bridge, inaugurated by a Russian czar,
spans the river in one breathtaking arc, its gold filaments jutting
out majestically from between the Grand and Petit Palaces.

In the morning light, Paris is stretching its muscles, as if about to take flight.

I leave the Right Bank and cross over the Seine via the Alexandre III Bridge. Inaugurated by a Russian czar, it spans the river in one breathtaking arc, its gold filaments jutting out majestically from between the Grand and Petit Palaces. The Viennese-style lamps stand at attention along both sides as I cross the water. The bridge curves upwards beneath my feet; a promise of flight which never quite fulfills itself. I pass the laughing gold horses that stand guard over the bridge, and am set down again at the foot of the gilded dome of Les Invalides.

It takes some time to appreciate this majestic esplanade leading to the final resting place of Napoleon I; the vast, uninterrupted stretch of lawn, the fringe of lime trees, the huge expanse of sky. Here the sun rules without hindrance, stretching across its domain—between the Seine, the stiff point of the Eiffel Tower, and the enormous gilded knoll of the dome that was built for the Sun King himself. I watch as a slow, dignified procession of clouds begins to travel across a deep blue carpet of sky unequalled anywhere else in the capital.

With such an auspicious introduction to Parisian nobility, I decide to press my advantage and pay my respects to the Faubourg Saint-Germain. Here, from the Regency to the Revolution, the aristocracy ruled with supreme composure and a sense of their own eternal belonging. Between rues Varenne and Grenelle, magnificent residences and superb gardens curtsey or bow side by side, not without some bustling, but each with their place in the sun.

On the rue de Grenelle, I imagine the witty conversation that could once be overheard in the neo-classic Hôtel du Châtelet, built for one of Voltaire's countess friends. Or at number 10, rue de Dominique, where Madame du Deffant received Montesquieu, Voltaire, and D'Alembert in her salon. Or a more salacious setting at number 57, where the Princesse de Monaco drifted apart from her husband and into the arms of the Comte de Condé, who lived at the Palais Bourbon.

Before the revolution, the area was also popular with foreign nobility, who brought rare and exclusive tastes to the neighborhood. Broad-shouldered, brocade-uniformed soldiers from the Urals guarded the entry to the Russian Embassy, while the ambassador and his guests dined on fish from the Baltic and caviar from Archangelsk.

Today, the Faubourg's sense of self-importance is no longer nourished by blue blood, but by one of its nearest modern equivalents, that of the ministers who serve the Republic. The elaborately wrought gates of the various ministries established in the neighborhood give an air of grandeur, and perhaps a *soupçon* of subterfuge to the political maneuvering that goes on behind them.

On rue de Varenne, I pass the Hôtel de Gouffier de Thoix, a sumptuous, playful *rocaille* façade, seemingly made of glittering sand, which stands behind a vast and imposing gateway, facing the prime minister's Matignon residence and the largest private gardens in Paris.

After so much inaccessible grandeur, the pure lines of the Four Seasons fountain, thrown into relief by the sharp morning sun, are a refreshing sight. This shows Paris as a haughty queen, flanked by the bearded Seine and the puny Marne. Voltaire, however, didn't think much of this fountain; he said it was a lot of stone for very little water.

Long after Voltaire passed away, but in a spirit he might have recognized, the most famous intellectuals of the twentieth century filled the cafés of boulevard Saint-Germain with new, fiercely-debated ideas.

In Saint-Germain, near the old church, the air once rang with the slogans, manifestos, and watchwords of the European intelligentsia. Exiled and resident artists, writers, filmmakers and intellectuals met here, orbiting around each other, moving through shifting epicenters of artistic affiliation and reaction. The cafés on this street became studies, theaters, salons, and observatories.

Intellectual revolution was declared in the 1930s across the tables of Les Deux Magots on the boulevard Saint Germain two decades after political revolution was plotted by the exiled Lenin and Trotsky in the Montparnasse cafés further south. In 1939, the focus of attention shifted to the Café de Flore. Picasso and André Breton set things off, attracting a host of other renowned or aspiring painters and writers. A year later, when it became the home-away-from-home of Sartre and de Beauvoir, the air was thick with existential angst. It was around this time too, that Heidegger exchanged the mists of the Rhine for the smoke-filled jazz cellars of Saint-Germain.

I peer through the window of another café that once played host to the intellectual and artistic élite of the day: the Brasserie Lipp, with its wood paneling, porcelain tiles, and mosaic of macaws and bizarre plants. Before the day fills the café with noise and movement, it looks like an exotic hideaway, submerged in the green shadows of some tropical swamp.

But the heyday of the cafés is long gone. The "isms" that were the buzzwords of the present have become the catchwords of the past. Those words, flung from table to table with so much vigor have come down to us in a more sober form, set in print and placed in alphabetical order on shelves. You'll find them in the few bookshops still holding out against the rising tide of tourists. They share something of a siege mentality.

I step inside the bookstore La Hune for a moment, watching booklovers browse the shelves: a frowning scholar picks up a slim volume of poetry, while a browser looks for escape between the covers of a new novel. I pick up a polemical essay just arrived from the offices of a nearby publisher, still clinging to its share of a shrinking market, still laying its money on the virtues of wit and intelligence. As I flip through the pages, I hear the spirits of Saint Germain debating with each other.

Rue de Verneuil, 7th arrondissement

Hotel Verneuil

Saint-Germain-des-Près and rue du Cherche-Midi guarded by César's Centaur statue, 6th arrondissement

In Saint-Germain, near the old church, the air once rang with the slogans, manifestos, and watchwords of the European intelligentsia... But the heyday of the cafés is long gone. The "isms" that were the buzzwords of the present have become catchwords of the past.

I walk up towards the Jardin du Luxembourg, passing in front of the towering church of Saint-Sulpice. The square in front of the church is fresh, youthful, Italianate; animated by the dazzling water spurting out of the fountain and the flurries of pigeon wings. It always feels like spring here. I move on, looking deep into the soft shadows of rue Servandoni and rue Garancière—catching tantalizing glimpses of exquisite antiques nestling in the golden half-light of the galleries, where paintings line up like windows within windows, views into the infinity of other countries and eras.

Italy also perfumes the air in the Jardin du Luxembourg, which was designed and built at the behest of Marie de Medici. People come here to breathe easier, to see some greenery, or to slow their pace of life for a moment before heading back into the street. Although there is plenty of opportunity for serious statue-spotting, many find the least classical figures of most interest: *Student Reclining with His Book, Feet Crossed on a Rusty Chair*; *Student Pretending Not to See the Watercolor Painter*; and, best of all, *Student Deigning to Bestow a Smile on the Watercolor Painter, Who in Turn Pretends Not to See Him, and Feigns Deep Interest in a Nearby Game of Chess.*

I leave this mute Arcadian sideshow behind me, to stand in the shadow of the trees, watching the haze of the fountains in the distance, the intense colors of the highly-manicured flower beds, the patterns in the gravel walkways, and the Fine Arts students passing by with cardboard sleeves full of sketches tucked under their arms. I might be a figure from a painting by Watteau…were it not for the kiosks selling the brightly-colored balls, windmills, buckets and spades which keep children busy once they have finished their sticky pink cotton candy.

I walk towards the exit which comes out onto the boulevard St-Michel—or the boul'Mich, as it is affectionately known—past Stendhal and Georges Sand, commemorated in stone. A sudden blast of traffic wipes out the calm—the birdsong, the shouts of

The Panthéon is one of those sepulchral monuments that ends up having a sort of oppressive magnetism,
like the clinging vestige of a nightmare...

Passage du clos Bruneau - Rue des Carmes

children, the spouting fountains and rustling trees—that I have just left behind. I prepare myself to enter a world where prestigious intellectual institutions line up back-to-back; a world of ideas, precision, exams, and footnotes.

The Latin Quarter. In these roads slotted in between the Sorbonne and the Seine, students sit with friends on the terraces of cafés, trying to act debonair and mature beyond their years, allowing themselves just one more coffee, just one more cigarette before they dive back into their books in the libraries. Further down towards Saint Michel, the streets become noisier, narrower, more medieval, with their street-food smells and hawkers shouting out their wares. But it's a far cry from the days when students really did speak Latin in the Latin Quarter: a time when Rabelais began the study of medicine, which gave him a wealth of raw material for his writing.

One of his favorite satirical subjects was the Sorbonne, that self-styled last bastion of academia. It remained largely unchanged until the unforgettable, carnivalesque events of May 1968, when students barricaded the streets and shook the institutions of French academic life to their core. Barricades, revolutions, demonstrations—these have shaped some of the most important changes the capital has seen. Today, it's not uncommon to come across banners and megaphones in the streets of Paris. The street is still a forum for open debate: people march to show that they want others to change with the times, and to show that the times need changing.

I walk on past the imposing Panthéon, which houses the remains of some of France's greatest men and women—Voltaire, Rousseau, and more recently, Pierre and Marie Curie. Set on a huge, deserted square, it is one of those sepulchral monuments that ends up having a sort of oppressive magnetism, like the clinging vestige of a nightmare. A funereal silence surrounds it.

I head down towards the river, after a brief pause in the tranquility of the Roman Arènes de Lutèce, to watch a group of men in civvies playing boules, the French equivalent of bocce ball, on the sandy ground. I pass the high white walls of the Paris Mosque, with its minaret and enticing Alhambresque patio, where students and locals sip sweet mint tea under the palm trees. A gust of steam floats out from the hammam (the baths), merging with the hot, humid air outside.

My last stop before the river is the Jardin des Plantes, with its manicured gardens and provincial atmosphere. Opposite, the Austerlitz train station taunts the dusty dinosaur skeletons and tragic orangutans, who can't escape the Natural History museum and the menagerie nearby. From here, I am drawn back along the quays to Notre Dame.

Notre-Dame is still glorious—a masterpiece of medieval craftsmanship, despite so many radical transformations. During the French Revolution, the cathedral was converted into a "Temple of Reason," and all the statues of the kings of Judah on the façade were systematically destroyed by the rabble; the revolutionaries thought they represented the kings of France. The nineteenth century saw Quasimodo and his beloved Esmeralda move in, thanks to Victor Hugo, along with the grimacing gargoyles that give the façade a touch of the grotesque.

There are still as many reasons to visit as there are busloads of tourists: the spectacle of sightseers from the farthest-flung reaches of the globe pouring forth en masse is quite astonishing. It opens up a microcosm of free trade, with foreign hawkers touting souvenirs of non-existent places to foreign tourists, like the street sign for a wholly imaginary "Place Tour Eiffel" that I once saw here.

I go inside the church. To the birds tucked among the flying buttresses under the roof, who look down through the great soaring arches, I'm a black dot. In the transept, the north end of the church, I am transfixed by a sublime rose-shaped window. It whorls and unfurls like a living flower, its stained glass a magnificent imperial purple.

I leave the murky light, the muffled echoes of the footsteps and whispers of the crowds of people moving around the nave, and come out again, blinking, on the square in front of the cathedral. A few steps farther on, and I reach kilometer zero. The whole of France is measured from this point. In the middle of the Île de la Cité, right in the center of Paris, is where France begins, putting out feelers that extend along the four points of the compass.

Next to it is a moving reminder that not all of us choose our own road: the Monument to the Deported. Inside, the walls of the crypt-like tunnel are covered with thousands of points of light—the lights of the souls that were extinguished in the concentration camps. The inscription reads: Forgive. Do not forget.

I move on past the green bookstalls lined up along the Seine, touting dusty hardbacks and dog-eared paperbacks, faded comic books, neat sheets of stamps and coins, quaint 30s pornography, yellowing sheet music, reproductions of famous paintings, and paintings of Paris in lively colors. The booksellers stand or sit on folding chairs, protective of their wares, in any weather. Their response to your purchase is unpredictable: despondency is as likely as enthusiasm.

I browse through a pile of paperbacks and bring out a copy of James Joyce's *Ulysses*. Its pages take you on a walk through a city with a very different character, Dublin. In there somewhere, however, is a reference to "Paris: the well-pleased pleaser." This book to end all books was finished and first published in Paris in 1922 by Sylvia Beach, founder of the original Shakespeare and Company

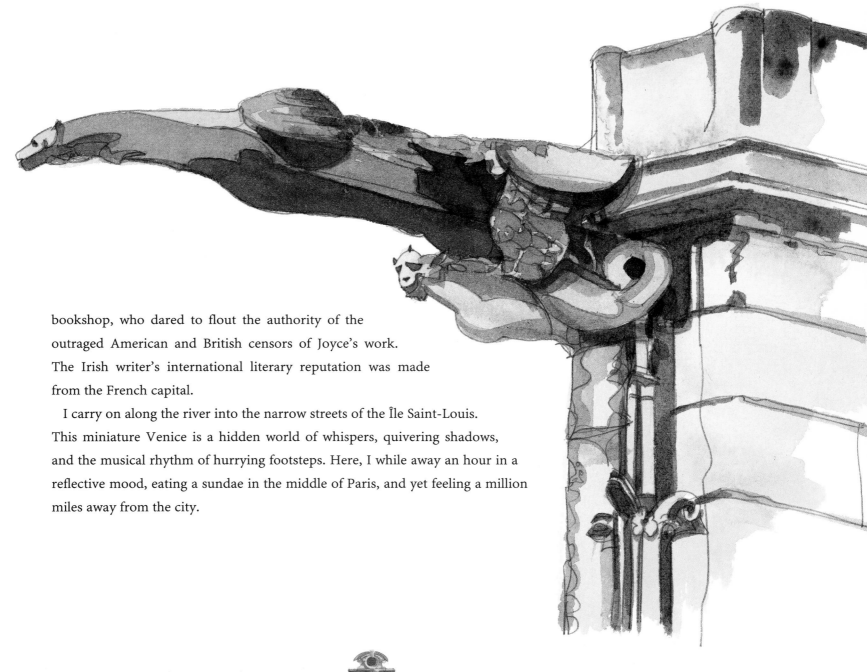

bookshop, who dared to flout the authority of the
outraged American and British censors of Joyce's work.
The Irish writer's international literary reputation was made
from the French capital.

    I carry on along the river into the narrow streets of the Île Saint-Louis.
This miniature Venice is a hidden world of whispers, quivering shadows,
and the musical rhythm of hurrying footsteps. Here, I while away an hour in a
reflective mood, eating a sundae in the middle of Paris, and yet feeling a million
miles away from the city.

The sublime rose-shaped window whorls and unfurls like a living flower, its stained glass a magnificent imperial purple.

The birds tucked among the flying buttresses under the roof look down through the great soaring arches…
A few steps farther on, I reach kilometer zero.

Square du Vert-Galant and the equestrian statue of Henri IV

This miniature Venice is a hidden world of whispers,
quivering shadows, and the musical rhythm of hurrying footsteps.

RESTAURANT

RESTAURANT *Paul* RESTAURANT.

15

Chez Paul, place Dauphine

The pont des Arts, overlooking the Seine, facing the Île de la Cité

Paris in the Afternoon

FROM THE ÎLE SAINT-LOUIS TO OPÉRA

An accordionist is playing nostalgic French *chansons* as I cross the bridge connecting the narrow Venetian streets of Île Saint-Louis with its larger, more powerful twin, the Île de la Cité. Now, I am at the heart of Paris, between these two islands that force the Seine to part on either side of them. I walk among the unshakeable, massive stone walls and turrets of the Île de la Cité's historic centers of power to the far end of the island, where it tapers to a long point.

Lured into the inviting brick and stone triangle of place Dauphine, I take a moment to savor a menu set in the window of the famous restaurant, *Chez Paul,* an imaginary meal I round off with a triangle of exquisitely creamy Camembert from the mouth-watering cheese board. Henry IV had this three-sided piazza built in honor of the dauphin (then the future Louis XIII). It has seen some royal frivolity in its time—not least of which was the extravagant doorway built entirely of sugar in honor of Louis XIV and Marie-Thérèse. In the last century, it was given a new connotation, this time spicy rather than sugary, by the Surrealist André Breton, who called it the pudendum of Paris.

I walk on, keeping clear of the hooves of Henri IV's horse as they paw the air, full of fighting spirit. The original statue was dismembered during the French Revolution; fragments of it can be seen in the Marais at the Musée Carnavelet, which chronicles the history of Paris. Further along, the elegant, slender arches of the pont Neuf link the two sides of the island to the opposite banks of the Seine. Its name might mean the New Bridge, but it is, in fact, the oldest Parisian bridge of them all. And just beyond the bridge, at the tip of the island, is the gently pointed apex of the Square du Vert Galant, a secret, shady hiding place. The fountain sparkles, while couples hold hands and forget the outside world beneath the weeping willow trees. There is a delicate hint of sin, an ironic sweetness in the air.

I cross the pont Neuf to the Left Bank and make my way towards the majestic cupola of the Institut de France, where outstanding

French intellectuals are honored with pomp and white-linen dinners, and borrowed foreign words are banished from the pages of modern *dictionnaires*. I turn my back on its grand semi-circular forecourt and step up onto the wooden pont des Arts, of a simpler and more modest design. The noise of the roaring traffic along the quays fades. Only bipeds (and quadrupeds on leashes) may enter here. The bridge is a popular hangout for musicians, students, and young Parisians.

The dark wood is burnished and hot beneath my feet. Through the cracks between the planks, I can see the Seine swirling past— a fascinating green, muscular body of water. I stop to lean on the balustrade and watch a flat-bottomed barge slowly motor past, long and tipped up at the end like a shiny black shoe. It moves along low in the water, loaded down with heaps of gleaming black coal. At the end is a small cabin where the family lives, and just enough space on the deck for their car. Behind me, a busker, red-faced and sweltering in the sun, is playing the bagpipes while groups of impromptu picnickers sit in chattering clusters on the ground. On the benches, pensive smokers sit contemplating the vast stretch and curve of the river. I cross to the opposite side of the bridge, where the mute, pale and perfect colonnades of the Louvre begin.

I step through a cool, shadowy archway into the Louvre's dazzling main forecourt, where a huge glass pyramid pokes out of the ground, flanked by miniature versions of itself. The Louvre is a place which has always erred on the side of excess. In winter you can forget the gloom of the shortening days by losing yourself in gallery after gallery of famous paintings and sculptures. But today, the sun has a more seductive appeal. The mummies have waited thousands of years for me to call and pay my respects— surely they'll wait another season. I stroll among the arcades instead, catching a glimpse of the twisting, white-marble torsos of antique gods on my way out.

The Café Marly facing the Louvre Pyramid

Porte Napoléon, Musée du Louvre

I cross into the Palais Royal gardens, where people are sitting in a circle around the fountain, reading or just people-watching. I catalogue the many different, enjoyable ways there are of idling away a sunny afternoon in a park in Paris. Observation is *de rigueur* here. It's a fine art and a grand tradition upheld by Colette, who filled a novel with what she saw in these gardens (her windows looked out onto them). She was one of many luminaries to have regularly frequented the most prestigious restaurant in Paris: Le Grand Véfour, at the foot of the gardens. So much was her appreciation of its culinary creations, that even when she became too ill to leave her apartment, she would ask to hear what was on the menu every day, and comment on it in her rich Burgundy accent.

I come to Buren's famous (or perhaps notorious?) black and white columns, like different lengths of stone sticks, set on the site of a former car park. Their shape may sound unintriguing, but they'll win you over in the end with their sci-fi fusion of the alien and the familiar. They remind me of rows of landing lights, waiting to guide an intergalactic mother-ship to its berth.

I turn onto the rue de Rivoli, diving into the cool shade of the stone arcades. Here, walking is a harmonious experience; my steps are a sequence of small curves, echoing the high sweep of each giant two-legged arch. I stroll past the eminent busts set into the walls of the Louvre, and past the wood-paneled English-language bookstore, where books are carefully retrieved with the help of ladders. The texts are rare, precious islands in a balmy sea of French.

I turn away from the street into a soothing tunnel of silence, the Galerie Vero-Dodat. This elegant covered arcade, bathed in iridescent light, is nearly two centuries old. It has an intimate feel, with its tiny, hidden curiosity shops, such as the violin-maker's and Capia's antique store, with its famous dolls, itself an antique at 175 years of age. A few steps farther on, I come to Galerie Vivienne, my heels clicking over the coats of arms, anchors, crosses, and stars scattered on the patterned floor.

The last row of arcades brings me to Angelina's, where I stop for a cup of the thickest, richest, most delicious hot chocolate in the world. With its pale ivory walls, its neat lines, and the fascination of whatever is reflected thousand-fold in the mirrors and windows, Angelina's is an ideal place to watch people who are busier than you are as they bustle by. In the distance are the gates of the Tuileries, and the park's restful lime trees and lawns are a muted green blur from here.

My favorite arcades are here in the Marais, in Henri IV's place Royale. It was renamed the place des Vosges in 1800 under Napoleon, after the first region of France to pay its share of the expenses of the revolutionary wars. These thirty-six symmetrical brick and stone mansions, nine for each side of the square, represent a masterpiece of mathematical rigor; yet there is nothing more charmingly human. In this square, Louis XIII took Anne of Austria to be his wife, in the presence of 1300 cavalrymen, 80 violinists, and 150 trumpeters. Madame de Sévigné also lived here in part of what is now the Musée Carnavalet, and not so far from Marion Delorme, who achieved a certain notoriety for her hundreds of lovers, including Cardinal Richelieu. Sometimes, she would dress up as a man for their clandestine trysts.

I try to retrace my steps, heading towards the Pompidou Center. I need to cast away from the banks of the Seine, and find my way back through the labyrinthine streets of the Marais. But however well I think I know the area, there always comes a point when I realize I am lost, overcome by a feeling that I've never been here before, like the opposite of déjà-vu. The area's sudden, enriching changes of atmosphere make familiar places surprising every time you stumble across them: like the intimate and hidden place du Marché Sainte Catherine, or, a few streets deeper into the Marais, the old Jewish Quarter, with its Mediterranean feel. On rue Vieille du Temple,

where people are sitting around the fountain...

I avoid the glare of the magnificently sardonic medusas on the gates of Hôtel Amelot de Bisseuil, where Beaumarchais organized a lucrative arms trade during the American War of Independence, and planned *The Marriage of Figaro*.

Le Centre Pompidou has an overwhelmingly optimistic feel to it. There are innumerable reasons to admire this twentieth-century icon, this industrial, cultural, palace of the people. The building's design is genuinely daring, surging assertively from the ground; its curves and colors are primitive and unashamed. The outside, reveling in the utility and practicality of its brash color-coded pipes and ducts, gives little clue to the stunning artworks contained within. And once you find yourself caught up in those unstoppable tubes, the ground beneath your feet quakes with the promise of takeoff for a more vigorous society.

I glide up the transparent escalator to the 6th floor, and stop for a refreshing drink in the *Georges* restaurant, where rays of sun fall across the clean-cut modern lines of the tables. From here, Paris spreads out like an immense patterned tablecloth at my feet.

From the Pompidou I head for another brash, popular building: the glitzy Cirque d'Hiver, a paradise for children. On the outside it looks like a cake, while inside, you find all the ingredients of the primitive magic of the circus: the terror of the roll of the drum and the crack of the whip. The spectacle reminds me to move on to the Père Lachaise cemetery, that great haphazard city of the dead. Once, down an avenue I will probably never find again, I stumbled upon the tomb of a long-forgotten lion tamer, with a design showing him on a happier day, riding on the back of the lion that ultimately killed him.

The hallowed bones of some of the most illustrious figures ever to have ended their days on French soil are neighbors at Père Lachaise: Molière, La Fontaine, Balzac, Proust, and Colette are here somewhere, along with Oscar Wilde, who died in disgrace, poverty and exile in a shabby hotel after his fall from glory as the toast of London's West End. I could spend hours here, paying my respects to Sarah Bernhardt, to Chopin, to Modigliani, strolling quietly amidst the shady avenues and crumbling tombs. The simple graves stand out because of their modesty; most are ornate mausoleums, decorated with statues, plaques, porcelain portraits, inscriptions, winged messengers and angels. Some corners are entirely forgotten—ivy pushes its way into cracks and tree roots push up under tombstones and set them aslant, while others are carefully tended, brightened with commemorative bunches of flowers or eccentric tokens left by admirers. Père Lachaise is a good place to reflect on posterity: what it makes of glory, and of memory.

From here, the Metro takes me to Montmartre, above ground. For the passengers watching the iron girders arch up and down, Paris is seen as if from a fairground ride. For those walking between the wide supporting columns below, the elevated train resembles an aqueduct, transporting the flow of people whose lives irrigate the dusty city streets. The train rumbles across northern Paris, and we look down onto the Canal St-Martin, where people line up for the arthouse cinema on the quay, passing the rows of black platform roofs at the Gare de l'Est, before swooping underground again at Barbès, as I strain for a last glimpse of the sky.

I resurface at Montmartre, and make my way towards the sugary white confection that is Sacré-Cœur. You can't miss it. Standing with my back to the basilica, I am at the highest point in the city, set in its cluster of hills, with a panoramic, exhilarating view over the whole metropolitan sprawl. From here, I can easily pick out the great landmarks which make the skyline so unmistakably Parisian. Some of their shapes are enigmatically alphabetical: the letter A of the Eiffel Tower, the H of Notre Dame, the n of the great gleaming modern arch at La Défense to the west, or the Roman Numeral clusters of the colorful high-rise blocks that one can see to the east.

Perched on its steep butte, Montmartre is a place that harbors both cliché—from Maurice Utrillo's platitudinous daubs to the tourist-trap portrait painters of place du Tertre—and artistic pedigree: Cubism was invented here in an old piano factory by Picasso, Braque, and Juan Gris.

I pass the Château des Brouillards, which was compared to a villa in Pompeii by its one-time occupant, the poet Gérard de Nerval. Montmartre, however, is more of a rabbit warren—both above and underground—as the narrow streets of houses are built on abandoned plaster of Paris quarries. The Lapin Agile is an appropriate name, then, for the bar in Montmartre where Edith Piaf and company wowed the crowds. Up here, between the symbolic rows of vines and the studios of the greatest artists of the century, some unholy reveling went on, shaking the fragile foundations. The Parisian coat of arms, with its motto Liberty, Alacrity, Vivacity, fluttered as the aperitif glasses glinted in the sun.

I move on from Montmartre to Pigalle, and to the vast boulevard de Clichy, where the air is thick with the discordant roar of traffic. This is the spot once graced by the jovial and fiery dancers of Jean Renoir's *Moulin Rouge*. The emblem of the underbelly of Paris, Pigalle combines the grace of the subjects portrayed in paintings by Nattiez or Fragonard with the boisterous and shocking boldness of the cancan dancers and their swishing skirts.

But Pigalle is not Pigalle anymore: the red-light district is now everywhere and nowhere. Explicit lingerie stores and sex shops line the boulevards: something once forbidden and secretly desired is now on permanent and anesthetizing display. The spice of guilty pleasures is too readily available to have much flavor any more, while eroticism makes its last stand in the heart of Pigalle, at 72, boulevard de Clichy, in the melancholy form of a museum.

I take off in search of a more magical place, the sloping, secretive place Saint-Georges. In the middle of the square, there is a statue of Gavarni, painter of so many *demi-mondaines* and ladies of the night. On the other side is the Hôtel de la Païva, private residence of the Marquise de Païva, *née* Thérèse Lachmann, a beautiful and scintillating young woman, who had a particular genius for winding men around her little finger. She lived on the ground floor of this neo-Renaissance mansion, where lions and angels writhe around the youthful figure of Abundance, depicted with swaying hips and a horn-of-plenty snaking up her arm, her hair held back with what appears to be the shell on which Venus rose from the waves.

I carry on through Nouvelle-Athènes—once home to George Sand, Chopin, Géricault, and Delacroix—and call at the Musée Gustave Moreau, where the artist used to live. He seems to have spent his entire life renewing his betrothal to the Queen of the Bizarre, in an atmosphere of silence bathed in the eerie, viscous sunlight of a fairy tale, in a dream tainted by opium or restless, half-waking sleep. He devoted the last years of his life to constructing his own museum, for posterity. Visiting it is a little like entering a vast wood-paneled theater, plunged in shadow, with occasional flashes of ceremonial splendor. Afterwards, you realize it is not a museum, after all: it is a secret temple, devoted to an ailing deity, a place governed by a different notion of time.

Several streets down, time is what seems to be most lacking, as I am swept up in the rush of weary commuters pouring into the Gare Saint Lazare. Above their heads, the huge station clock moves its hour and minute hands with the same inexorability as the pointing arms of the guards inside, as train after train glides away from the platform and gathers speed towards the suburbs. Time is unstoppable; trains will leave with or without their passengers.

In front of the station, everyone chooses the same meeting point, the foot of Arman's sculpture of a heap of clocks, *Temps pour Tous*, Time for Everyone—but is there enough to go around? Standing beneath this totem pole of time, I am surrounded by the hurrying feet of passengers past, present, and future. I imagine Madame Bovary arriving on the train from Le Havre to spend a precious, illicit hour or two in the arms of a mid-ranking manager, who neglects to tell her that he is married.

I push on, through the crush of people rushing in and out of the department stores on Boulevard Haussmann, toward Opera Garnier and the streets of foreign tourist boards, travel agencies and banks which radiate out from its steps.

The rue de Rivoli arcades

ANGELINA

ANGELINA

Jardin des Tuileries

*The Palais Royal Gardens and
Daniel Buren's columns*

Buren's famous columns remind
me of rows of landing lights,
waiting to guide an intergalactic
mother-ship to its berth.

The place des Vosges in the heart of the Marais

The place des Vosges is a magical square: thirty-six houses of brick and stone, four times nine—
a masterpiece of mathematical rigor; yet there is nothing more charmingly human...

Place des Vosges

Rue Vieille du Temple: Medusa head sculpted on the doors of the Hôtel Amelot de Visseuil (above)
and a mosaic sign nearby (right)

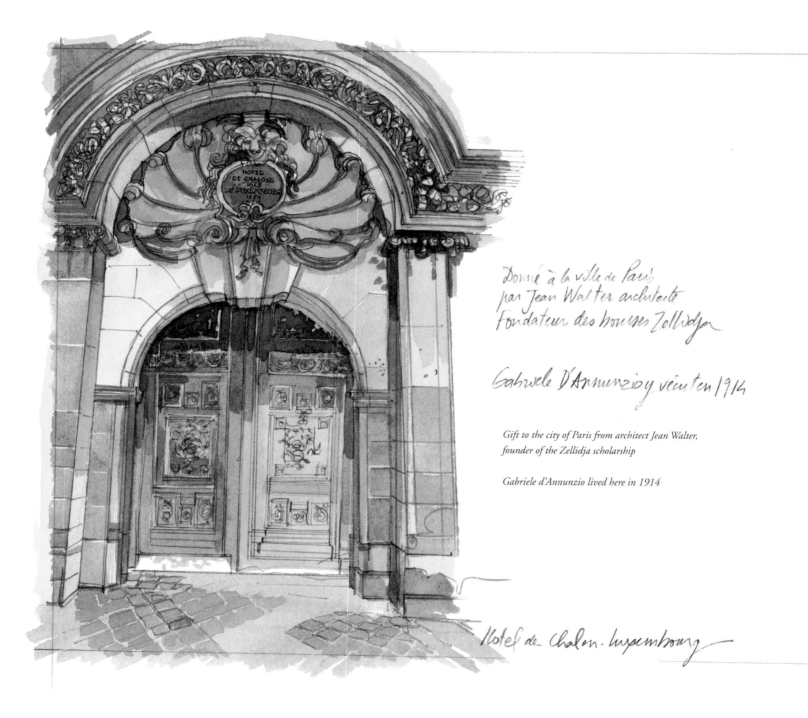

Donné à la ville de Paris
par Jean Walter architecte
Fondateur des bourses Zellidja

Gabriele D'Annunzio y vécu en 1914

*Gift to the city of Paris from architect Jean Walter,
founder of the Zellidja scholarship*

Gabriele d'Annunzio lived here in 1914

Hôtel de Chalon-Luxembourg

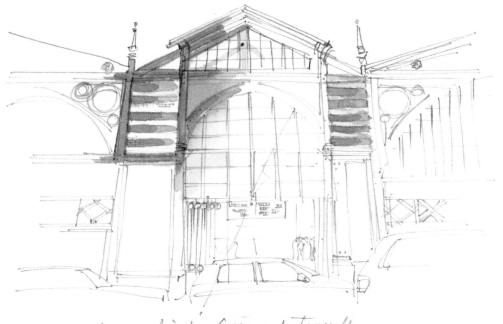

ECOLE SUPÉRIEURE
D'ART APPLIQUÉ
DUPERRÉ

le marché du Caveau du Temple
est ouvert du mardi au
Samedi de 9ʰ à 12ʰ30

*The Caveau du Temple market is open Tuesday–Saturday
from 9:00 a.m.–12:30 p.m.*

le caveau du temple

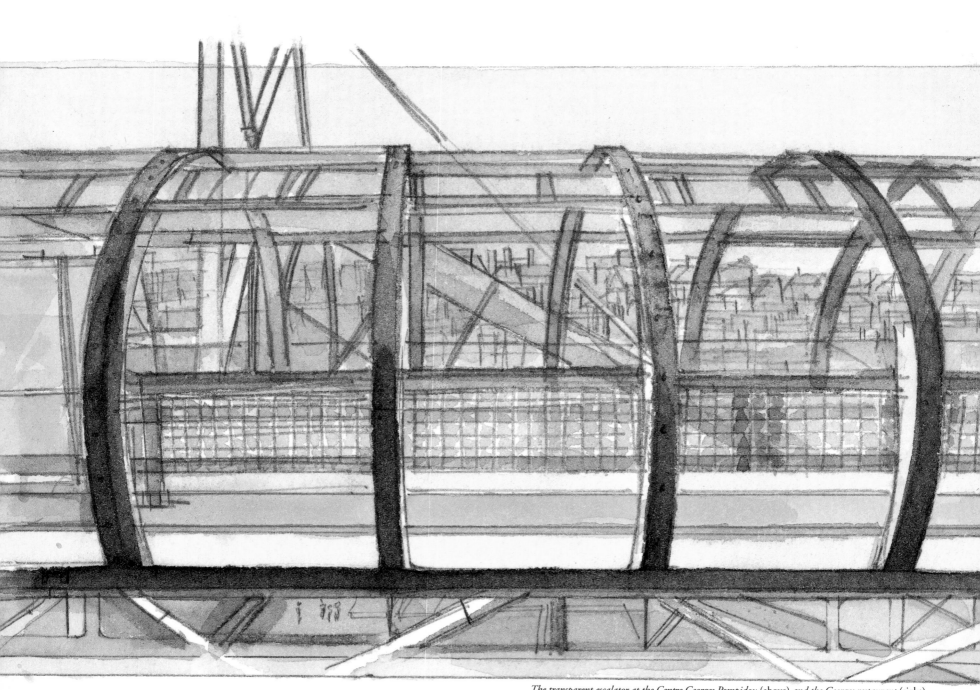

The transparent escalator at the Centre Georges Pompidou (above) *and the Georges restaurant* (right)

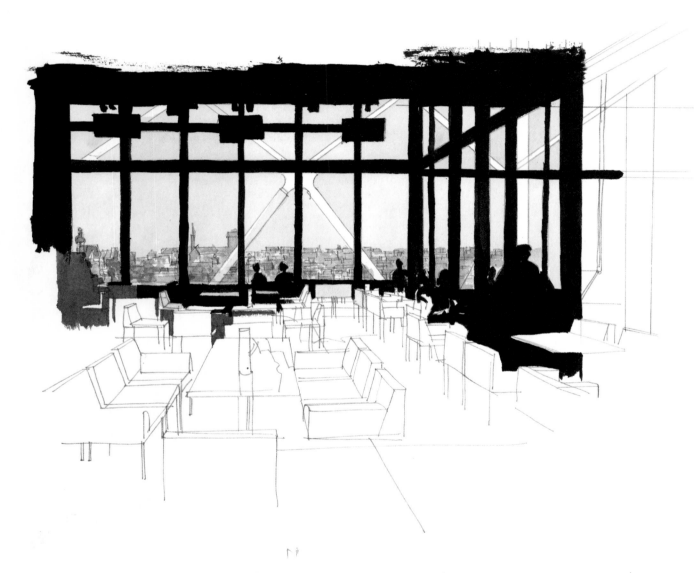

The Pompidou Center surges assertively from the ground; its curves and colors are primitive and unashamed.

"Egyptomania" on the rue Beaubourg, behind the Centre Georges Pompidou

The glitzy Cirque d'Hiver, a paradise for children,
with all the primitive magic of the circus:
the terror of the roll of the drum and the crack of the whip.

114 Rue Amelot
Paris 11ᵉ

Père Lachaise

Le Crème à Entiène

Max
ERNST
1891 - 1976

INGRES

ROMAN

CIESLEWICZ
1930-1996

8   317   306

29   318   307

Emile
CHARTIER
1868 - 1951

ALAIN

EMILE
CHAR

*The 19th arrondissement's town hall,
avenue de Laumière*

*The MK2 movie theatre, along the canal, on
the quai de la Seine, 19th arrondissement*

The "pont des suicidés" in the Buttes Chaumont Park

les Buttes Chaumont

Parisian "countryside," rue Mathurin Moreau and rue Edgar Poe, 19th arrondissement

Elevated metro above the boulevard de la Chapelle

Boulevard de Clichy

I move on from Montmartre to Pigalle, and to the vast boulevard de Clichy, where the air is thick with the discordant roar of traffic... But Pigalle is not Pigalle anymore—the red-light district is now everywhere and nowhere.

Perched on its steep butte, Montmartre is a place
that harbors both cliché—the portrait painters of
place du Tertre—and artistic pedigree: Cubism was
invented here in an old piano factory by Picasso,
Braque, and Juan Gris.

58–60 boulevard de Clichy

In front of the station, everyone chooses the same meeting point, the foot of Arman's sculpture of a heap of clocks, TEMPS POUR TOUS, TIME FOR EVERYONE—but is there enough to go around? Standing beneath this totem pole of time, I am surrounded by the hurrying feet of passengers past, present, and future.

122 rue de Provence, which used to house one of Paris's most famous brothels, the "One Two Two"

"LES CAHIERS"
de Condorcet

Lycée Condorcet, rue Pasquier, behind Saint-Lazare railway station

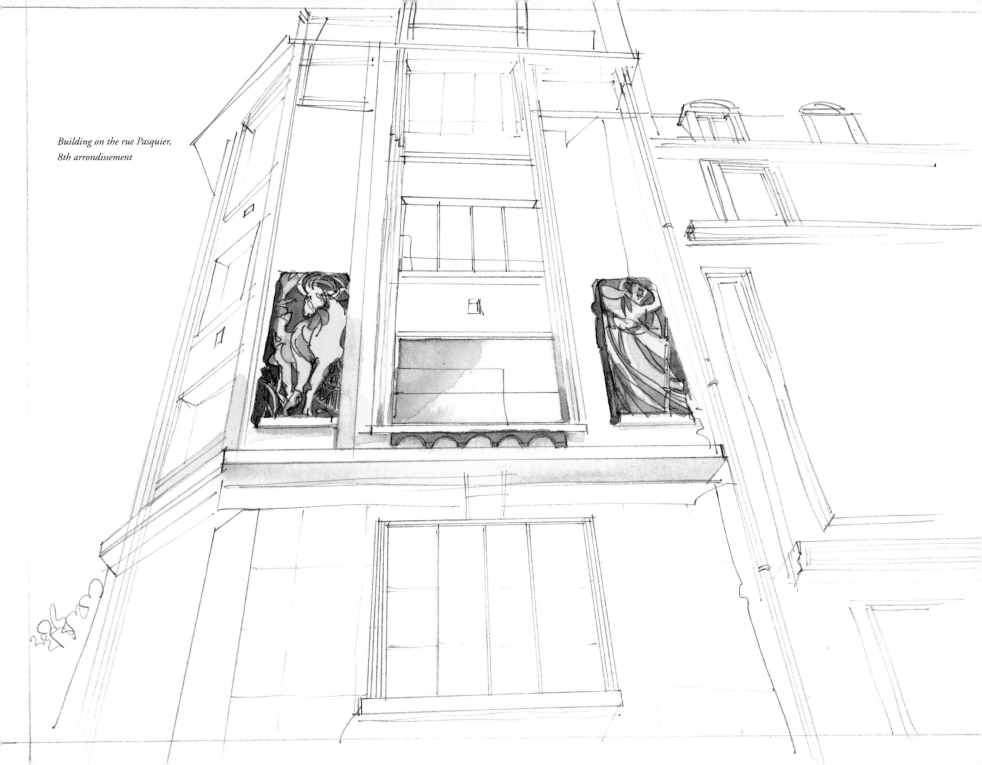

*Building on the rue Pasquier,
8th arrondissement*

The Dance *by Jean-Baptiste Carpeaux, on the façade*
of the Opéra Garnier

Above me, on the ornate façade (the work of 75 different sculptors), only Apollo appears unconcerned by the pressures of city life, as he bends time to his will, turning it into music. He plucks his lyre within earshot of the statues of Pegasus, but I suspect his skill is more for the benefit of Carpeaux's dancers. No doubt he is playing something suitably sensual: the naked white bodies of these women shocked the virtuous when they first appeared, caught up in their infinite erotic circle.

The opera house itself is an impressive luxury, dappled with exaggerated detail, a perfect celebration of the frenzied wheeling and dealing, as well as the fleshpots, of Napoleon III's reign. Inside, banks of glowing lights guide you to the curving, plush balconies—and the surprise of the 1964 Chagall ceiling with its floating dream figures in the auditorium. The city's magnificent ballets now take center stage here; operas are now performed at the ultra-modern Opéra Bastille, designed by architect Carlos Ott, since the 1990 opening of "Les Troyens" by Berlioz. I leave, making a graceful, sweeping exit down the grandest marble staircase in Paris.

petite ondée

Paris in the Evening

FROM THE EMBANKMENTS OF THE SEINE TO THE CHAMPS-ÉLYSÉES

Flanked by so many splendors, the river becomes quite timid...

Evening is my favorite time to visit the Eiffel Tower. At pont Neuf, I hop on a little boat that resembles a *vaporetto* and buzzes down the Seine. Flanked by so many splendors, the river becomes quite timid. Shrinking, turning in on itself, it hesitates between becoming a stream or a canal, and the water looks fake, almost like a painting of itself. On either side, the riverbanks whisper in turn, "Look!" "Go on!" "Come back!," their entreaties punctuated by the muffled cries of scavenging seagulls. In front of the boat, tiny, resplendent kingfishers zigzag across the river; they seem to open up the path ahead, pulling us up the river as if by invisible ropes.

We pass the Musée d'Orsay on the Left Bank, an immense building which was once a train station, with its statues of the cities of Bordeaux, Toulouse, and Nantes, and its two giant clock faces. These days, travelers headed for this station end their journey in the building itself, transported by a stunning collection of art from the second half of the nineteenth century. The original station was hardly finished before it became obsolete, overtaken by the advent of the electric train. Now, it has a more enduring function,

as a reservoir of the imagination. Orson Welles used it for his adaptation of Kafka's *The Trial*, making it a courtroom, a maze of archives, and a labyrinth filled with the dust of countless nightmares, where you might suddenly come across Romy Schneider showing her webbed fingers to Joseph K.

A little farther along, the boat passes the neo-Gothic American Church, then, on the right, there's just enough time to take in the silhouette of the Palais de Tokyo—with its slender white colonnade and statues of reclining nymphs—before it is superseded by the cold, neoclassic expanse of the Palais de Chaillot.

I step into the Trocadéro Gardens, where the double curve of blond limestone crosses the open square in a firm, decisive line, and descends to the great fountain, an impressive alliance of power and precision. It passes between the standing nudes: now, in the gloaming, their bronze, motionless footsteps echo the curve sweeping round them, reflecting the light like quicksilver.

Beyond them is the most powerful symbol in Paris, the brainchild of Monsieur Eiffel, neither beautiful nor ugly, just unique, self-evident, unforgettable. Standing between the dark, sculpted feet of the tower, you feel as small as a child looking up at a tall, authoritarian parent. Your eye is drawn irresistibly upwards to the tip of the needle hemming the lace of a passing cloud. You've seen it a thousand times in reproduction and now it finally stands before you, oversize rather than life-size, but nothing diminishes the power of the experience.

Massive and light, the tower crouches on the Earth as if about to fling itself upwards into space. It dominates the whole city with its vehement simplicity, its naked power. It also unites it—wherever you are, you can always find your bearings in relation to its black needle, pointing to your place on the page of the city.

I cross over Iéna Bridge, back to the Right Bank. Evening is on its way. This is the time of day when the Champs-Élysées, rushing down from Étoile to the Rond Point while the silent trees stand and watch, becomes worthier of its lofty name. Everything the avenue loses during the day to travel agencies, tourists, and the pallid monotony of commerce, it regains in this light, which gives it a fabulous Second Empire or Belle Epoque glow, purging it for an instant of the dingy smudge of the crowds.

All the suburban kids in the world seem to converge here, dragging themselves from one drugstore to another, passing longingly in front of the luxury boutiques and chain stores, affecting an arrogant blend of disdain and fascination. Every ten steps, a pounding disco beat thumps out of an air-conditioned hall. If Paris had a Fifth Avenue, this would be it.

There is no doubt that the Champs-Élysées still has a certain degree of glamorous appeal and hedonistic temptation. The cinemas look like they themselves should be on the silver screen: luxurious red-plush pleasure domes, named after ocean liners or great palaces—The Georges V! The Normandie! The UGC Triomphe! Or the opulent boutiques of the great French

The Île Saint-Louis viewed from the Seine

The Musée d'Orsay... These days travelers headed for this former train station
end their journey in the building itself.

designers—Louis Vuitton, Yves Saint Laurent. Or the elegant arcades—the Lido, the Claridge—haunted by the women, stylish to a fault, who still embody that irresistible Parisian chic. I remember how, as a child, passing beneath the bow window of the Guerlain building (the work of Ménès, an illustrious designer of ocean liners), the sight of a hand clad in a black glove could set me dreaming for days.

I reach the place de l'Étoile, where it always feels as if this must be it, your final destination, as if all roads would inevitably lead you here. Now called place Charles de Gaulle, its original name is still in use, as the best description of this vast radiating star. In that inimitable, adrenalin-fuelled Parisian way, cars careen around the imposing Arc de Triomphe, which stands like an impenetrable, oblivious island amid the tide of traffic. The fact that this was the world's first organized rotary may come as a surprise to any pedestrian foolhardy enough to attempt to cross it. I walk around the edge of the circle, crossing each of the twelve avenues in turn. On the Champs-Élysées side, I am inadvertently immortalized in any number of vacation photographs, while euphoric visitors pose wherever they can, framed by the great arch. I wish I could see how the pictures come out, back home, in so many different countries of the world.

The Arc de Triomphe sets down in stone the greatness of French history. Napoleon's stone monument echoes those of the Roman emperors and Louis XIV's Porte Saint-Denis. It houses the Tomb of the Unknown Soldier, recalling the moment when General de Gaulle stood in front of the Eternal Flame in August 1944, at the Liberation of Paris. The Arc de Triomphe is a monumental fragment in the epic mosaic of French history. Despite its solidity, something about its beauty is not quite real, not quite there. Strangely, it gains strength from celluloid; one of my most enduring memories of the arch is as the site of the execution of Simone Signoret at the end of the 1969 film, *L'Armée des Ombres*.

The streets, the buildings, and even the rooftops around the place Charles de Gaulle are teeming with producers—and many unforgettable scenes have been shot on location here. This was where the great French post-war film director, Jean-Pierre Grumbach, better known by the surname Melville, captured the essence of those improbable bars that never go out of fashion: they are the real stars of films like *Second Wind, The Samurai,* and *The Red Circle*. His fragile, nocturnal heroes are never far from the Étoile.

Farther down the Champs-Élysées, at number 25, I bump into the adventurous Marquise de Païva once more. She has gained more than just height in the move from place Saint-Georges. On the imitation Renaissance façade I can see how gallantry renews its attack, fidgeting, quivering, and carving its incisive curves around the two delightfully allegorical figures of a pair of hounds lying together. Only half a century separates the soldiers' powerful "*Marseillaise*"—which resounded around Étoile in 1792—and the construction of La Païva's residence: but in that time, the tide had turned a number of times.

Torn between alternate visions of France—between glory and success, between fame and honor, between revolutionary ideals and wealth—I finally reach the foot of the Champs-Élysées, and place de la Concorde, easily the most magnificent square in Paris. Vast crowds of Parisians came to the Concorde, originally called place Louis XV, to watch the joyful celebration of the marriage of the future Louis XVI and Marie Antoinette. Hundreds were crushed to death in the throng. And the marriage that began with such a tragedy was to end with the beheading of the royal couple, on the very same site—renamed place de la Révolution for the occasion—barely a quarter of a century later.

I reach the river just as the sun sets on Louis XIV, the Sun King, and Napoleon, over the esplanade of Les Invalides, the building's sphere glowing huge and red as the sun itself, then gradually disappearing as the dark blue velvet of night spreads across the sky and cloaks the skyline.

Les jardins du Trocadéro

Beneath the shadow of the Eiffel Tower's metal skirt I am taken back to my earliest childhood, when this myth, seen a thousand times in reproduction, was first presented to me life-size... On that first visit, and ever since, my eye has been drawn irresistibly, intoxicatingly upwards to the tip of the needle hemming the lace of a passing cloud.

vendeur de souvenirs. Notre-Dame

Place Tour Eiffel !! belle adresse !

Sign from a souvenir shop near Notre Dame featuring
the non-existant Place Tour Eiffel. Nice address!

The Champs-Élysées

Hermès

Kenzo

givenchy

Yves Saint Laurent

Luxury boutiques and glamorous stop-offs on the Champs-Élysées and the avenue George-V

Marius et Janette

Crazy Horse

Evening is on its way. This is the time of day when the Champs-Élysées, rushing down from Étoile to the Rond Point while the silent trees stand and watch, becomes worthier of its lofty name. Everything the avenue loses during the day to travel agencies, tourists, and the pallid monotony of commerce, it regains in this light…

The Champs-Élysées

Allons enfants

The place de la Concorde and the Obelisk from Luxor

The exact spot on the place de la Révolution, today's place de la Concorde, where the revolutionaries guillotined Louis XVI on January 21st, 1793

Paris at Night

FROM QUAI SAINT-BERNARD TO THE HOTEL CRILLON

Strangers in the night...

Quai Saint-Bernard at night

At nightfall throughout the summer, Parisians itch to leave their apartments and join the crowds of people out in the streets. Throughout the city, every café table on every *terrasse* is occupied, and coveted. The atmosphere fizzes with seduction and hilarity; words and wit are illustrated with curls of cigarette smoke from a gesturing hand.

I leave the busy tables behind—with their lean waiters who whisk in and out balancing round trays of glasses—and descend a flight of stone steps leading onto the walkways that line the banks of the Seine. Here, summer has a more intimate feel to it: couples sit and whisper to each other on stone benches, or lean over the parapets of majestic bridges, watching the currents eddying past.

Away from the glare of the streetlights above me, I become more sensitive to the many different, soft shades of light, as night spreads into yellow, purple, and black, like blotted ink. I pass the Institut du Monde Arabe, whose intricate glass and aluminum façade has thousands of tiny light-sensitive shutters that open and close according to the brightness of the day, a combination of high technology and the traditional Arab lattice-work known as *moucharabiyah*.

I reach the quai Saint-Bernard, which runs alongside the railings of the Jardin des Plantes's menagerie, transformed at night into a mysterious, shadowy world of rustling jungle shapes. It spreads out into the open-air sculpture garden inspired by the Hakone museum near Tokyo. Almost thirty artists committed to the ideals of abstract sculpture have come up with works to surprise, amuse or bemuse passersby on a summer evening. I pause in front of a dagger-like obelisk, watching its edges gleam in the lamp-light. This is a corner of the city which defines the essence of Paris—art, greenery, the Seine, the façades of the buildings—but which at the same time blends them into one indefinable whole.

I approach the first in a series of half-moon amphitheatres with tiered stone seats, molded out of the wide quay. I hear music. Tango. On these impromptu stages, whose front edges drop abruptly into the dark moving river, dancers press against each other in the warm, intimate darkness of the summer night. Dressed in sleek or shifting black, their legs intertwine and cross, casting evocative shadows. A boat glides past on the river, and suddenly projects its probing spotlight into the arena, just long enough to pick out a couple suspended in a symmetrical figure, before the bright light moves on and they whirl back into the semi-darkness. The nostalgia of the accordion, and the mournful, swooping violin may only be playing from a portable CD player, but there is something about this open-air tango that recalls the origins of the dance in the streets of Buenos-Aires.

Paris played a modest, but pivotal role in the development of tango over the last century or so—championing the dance when it was first exported, and encouraging its popularity throughout Europe and its credibility in Buenos Aires itself. It was in Paris, too, that the flame of the pure Argentinean form of the dance was kept alight in exile, when military rule back home made any kind of public meeting difficult. It seems to me that when danced in the French capital, it captures both the irresistible haughtiness and the open sensuality of Paris itself.

Hours are wiped from the clock as I sit here watching, absorbed, and filled with the sighs, suspense, and desire of the music. Farther up the river, in more secluded areas of the quays, the game of seduction enacted by the dancers on the quai Saint Bernard becomes more intense, as couples feverish with summer heat seek out the darkest and most intimate places, under bridges, away from the surveillance of street lamps. And still the boats glide past, suddenly catching them in flagrante delict with a gleeful finger-pointing searchlight.

Paul Verlaine called it), like Paris, builds a burlesque platform of eloquence beneath our feet.

I stumble back to the place de la Concorde as the first translucent pink light seeps out under the lid of the sky. The streetlamps go out one by one, as if my return were their cue to knock off for the day. Footsore, but inebriated after my twenty-four hour fix of the sights, sounds, smells and sensations of Paris, I am brought to an awed standstill at the sight of a woman in an evening dress leaning over a balcony at the city's most sumptuous hotel, the Crillon. She lifts a champagne flute, unsteadily, headily, as if to drink to my health—or so I think, until I see that she must be toasting something far grander: the majesty of the Seine as seen from her window, the symbol of the life and energy of a magnificent city.

I sigh in agreement. And wonder what time that corner café starts serving breakfast…

The pont des Arts at night

Open-air sculpture museum, quai Saint-Bernard

The menagerie in the Jardin des Plantes is transformed at
night into a mysterious, shadowy world of rustling jungle shapes.

I am brought to an awed standstill at the sight of a woman leaning over a balcony at the city's most sumptuous hotel, the Crillon.

The place de la Concorde tinted by dawn's first light

Love in Paris is a long-buried past that glitters as it is gradually exposed to
the light of day once more; it is the present, swiftly unfurling beneath our feet...

ACKNOWLEDGMENTS
This sketchbook is dedicated to C, to E, to F, to MJ and to S!
Thank you, of course, to Arches, Raphaël and to Winsor & Newton.

SELECTED BIBLIOGRAPHY
Baillie, Kate and Tim Salmon. *Paris: The Rough Guide*.
London: Rough Guides Ltd. (Penguin Group), 1995.

Jeuge-Maynart, Isabelle, ed. *Paris; Guides Bleus/Hachette Livre*.
Paris: Hachette Tourisme, 1999.

Murat, Laure, ed. *Paris des Ecrivains*.
Paris: Editions du Chêne, Hachette Livre, 1996.

Poisson, George. *Guide des Statues de Paris: Monuments, Décors, Fontaines*.
Paris: Editions Hazan, 1990.

Russell, John. *Paris*. New York: Harry N. Abrams, 1983.

IN THE SAME SERIES:
My Italian Sketchbook